101 Power Strategies

Tools to Promote Yourself as the Contractor of Choice

D1198299

by
Paul Montelongo

Edited and designed by:
Marilyn Schwader
clarityofvision@earthlink.net
Printed by:
Pine Hill Press
4000 West 57th Street
Sioux Falls, SD 57106-4228

Table of Contents

Dedication

To my family and friends who have endured with me through my entrepreneurial ventures over the years. Thanks for your support.

To all of the women and men in the construction industry that I have had the privilege of working with over the last 23 years. You have taught me a lot.

To you, the dedicated professional contractor who goes out day after day to make a buck. I know it is not easy, but it is entirely possible to be the *Contractor of Choice*.

Introduction

My desire is for you to become the *Contractor of Choice*. The title *Contractor of Choice* has a two-fold meaning. I want customers to choose you as their contractor. I also want you to be able to choose the sort of business you will operate. Hence, each strategy in this book can also be referred to as a "strategic choice." In addition, my desire is for you to re-think your entire marketing and promotion plan. In fact, I want you to reconsider the entire purpose of your enterprise. What do I mean by reconsidering the purpose of your enterprise? I want you to change your mindset about what you do for a living. You may be the most qualified technical expert in your industry. You might be the most efficient manager of people and resources. You may even be the industry's most productive salesperson. But when it comes right down to it, what business are you really in?

I suggest that you are in the marketing business. Every lead, every sale, every award-winning project you perform came because of some type of marketing effort. Without marketing and promotion of your enterprise, there was no phone call to your office that led to any of the above accomplishments. That is the mindset I want you to adopt from now on. You are in the marketing business. Every day, you must market and promote your business, your services, or yourself in order to see the results in the future. The remodeling projects and the new homes you build or the trade services you perform are all a by-product of your marketing and promotion efforts.

In the following pages, you will find *101 Power Strategies* for promoting your business. Some of these you may have already used. Many of these may be new or an expansion of concepts you are familiar with. In all cases, your marketing creativity and imagination will be teased and you will think of even greater ways to promote yourself as the *Contractor of Choice*.

Obviously, there are thousands of ways to promote your business. For every one strategy, there are hundreds of marketing sub-strategies. Your experience, your budget, and your willingness to take a risk determine the strategies you choose to use. However, you must start somewhere. I believe everything begins with your commitment to marketing. In these pages, I have attempted to set before you the most common and most effective means of promoting yourself in the contracting business. I have also provided many strategies that are not so common in our industry. Some strategies have been adopted from other industries. In order to qualify as a promotional strategy in this book, I assessed the strategies with the following criteria. The strategy:

✔ Must be relatively inexpensive. In most cases, an investment of under $500 will get you going. Many strategies are "no-cost" methods.

✔ Must have the capacity to make an impact in your business immediately, and over the long term.

✔ Must have been previously tried and tested in the construction industry, or can be easily applied to the industry.

✔ Must result in additional sales for you, which in turn means more money.

✔ Must be easy to quickly implement.

You will notice, too, that this book can be read in a very short period. Each *Power Strategy* has a short description of the concept. I want you to use all of your creative and imaginative capacity to implement the *Power Strategies* in this book. Here is a suggestion that I personally use. If you were to look at the books I have in my personal library, you would notice that each of them is full of notes in the margins, highlighted paragraphs, paper clipped pages, and dog-eared corners. That is because I *use* the books I read. Please do the same with this book. That will not offend me at all. In fact, it will be a compliment. This book is intended to get you thinking about your marketing strategy and mostly to get you moving in the right promotional direction. And finally, it is designed to help you make more money.

Section 1

Spread the
Word

Leon was the eldest son of eight children. At the impressionable age of nine, his out-of-style crew haircut, soft jelly-belly torso, and crooked front teeth caused him to be shy and self-conscious. For parents of a family this size, it was a real challenge to give the nurturing and attention that each child deserved. Deep inside, Leon was burning to be noticed, to promote himself as a special individual. And then one day, while on summer vacation with his family in the hot city of Houston, Texas, Leon would learn his first lesson in publicity.

Standing 5' above the chlorine-filled aqua-blue swimming pool on a diving board, Leon realized that if his attempt at a front somersault dive was to be noticed, he must advertise the upcoming event. Slightly bent over to study the impending dive maneuver, Leon had an idea. The quickest method of publicizing this momentous occurrence was to make a public declaration. Yes, advertising the event verbally with all of the volume Leon could muster would be a sure-fire way to get noticed. Leon knew that to get noticed would be important, but to get praised for his valiant dive would be the pinnacle of success, the real payment for his announcement.

With all of the lung capacity of a pre-pubescent weakling, Leon yelled at the peak of his voice from atop the diving board, "Hey everybody. Watch me! Watch me! Hey over there, watch me! Watch me do a somersault. Watch me everybody!" When Leon was certain that all eyes were on him, he slowly moved to the back of the diving board for a running start. Once more, he checked the audience to ensure their rapt attention. To be certain they were focused on Leon, he shouted one more time, "Watch me everybody!" Now was the time to deliver the goods. Leon ran to the front end of the diving board and leaped into the air as high as he could. Landing on the very front edge of the board, Leon was vaulted into the air. His somersault dive was the first of its kind... for Leon, that is. The splash at the end of the dive could have flooded the parking lot at that Houston motel. The style and grace of the dive was like a Longhorn steer in a Texas wine cellar. Leon didn't know the difference, for he had delivered on his announcement. He had done a somersault and everyone had seen him. Leon swam to the edge of the pool, climbed out, and began collecting on his publicity. Praise was showered on Leon from family, friends, and strangers. Leon had learned his first lesson in marketing. *Let everyone around you know what you do. Speak it. Shout it. Vocalize it.*

To verbalize what you do, your intentions, your products, and your services is the oldest and most certain method of promoting yourself as the *Contractor of Choice*. Sometimes it seems uncomfortable to tell everyone you know what you do. However, you are going to be asked many times in your career what you do. You must have an answer ready that inspires your listener to want to know more. The good news is that you can say it with style and people will listen. Think about the following *13 Power Strategies* and how you will implement them.

Strategy #1

Talk to Everyone You Know.

Talk to everyone you know and meet. Tell them that you are a contractor. Have a little excitement about what you do and what the benefits are of what you do. Excitement and enthusiasm are contagious. Think of friends, associates, or acquaintances that would benefit from your service and products. There is a principle in the network marketing industry called "the three-foot rule." In essence, it says that anyone who is within three feet of you should be approached and offered the opportunity to listen to your message. The law of averages are on your side when you spread the word. Knowing your product and what benefits you bring to the marketplace is important. Your ability to ask quality questions and to effectively listen to your customer's real needs creates all sorts of business opportunities. When one person listens to you and repeats your message to someone else, a synergy is created and eventually hundreds and maybe thousands will know of your service or product.

Strategy #2
Say it in an Elevator.

In the 30 seconds it takes to ride up to the 12th floor of your bank, can you describe exactly what you do and why you are the best contractor for the job? An "elevator speech," as it is sometimes called, must captivate the listener's attention and inspire them to want to know more about you. A persuasive "elevator speech" will be brief, approximately 30 to 45 seconds. The speech must be sincere, easy to remember, and easily repeatable by the listener. The speech should also stimulate an emotional response because it usually offers a benefit or solution to some relevant problem. The overall idea of an "elevator speech" is to generate an attraction to you so that you will be asked to further explain what you do.

In a seminar I gave recently, Robert was asked what he does for a living. Robert had this to say about his business, "I can be your best friend or I can be your worst enemy." Everyone's attention was instantly on Robert. Robert is a private investigator. He probes into the lives of couples who are getting divorced. He gathers information to be used by lawyers for divorce settlements. Depending on which spouse Robert represents, his description of his business is very accurate and interesting.

Strategy #3

Ask, Ask, Ask, and Ask Again.

You have the ability to achieve anything you wish if you will just gather the confidence and ask for what you want. You can ask a prospective client for an appointment. Ask a vendor or trade contractor for better service and discount pricing for more volume of work. Ask your banker for a better interest rate on your interim financing loans. Ask your employees to provide better service to your clients. Ask for the sale. Ask a direct question to a prospective client... "May I have your business? I am the best person for your job." Ask regularly and ask in different ways. Asking will require that you get out of your comfort zone. However, persistence will pay huge dividends.

In their brilliant best seller, *The Aladdin Factor*, Jack Canfield and Mark Victor Hansen challenge you to believe that anything is possible if you dare to ask. These men should know, for they are the authors of the phenomenal *Chicken Soup for the Soul®* book series. To date they have sold over 60 million *Chicken Soup* books. I highly recommend *The Aladdin Factor* for your personal and professional library.

Strategy #4

Ask for Referrals.

This simple strategy may be the most profitable you will ever employ. No matter what your business or trade, ask for referrals from your current clients and customers. This strategy has the potential of increasing your business two-fold, or even three-fold. Your clients are already aware of your service and product. They will promote you for free. All they have to do is spread the word. However, they need your assistance. You must remind them. You must ask for at least three leads from every client.

When asking for a referral, make certain that your customer is completely happy with your service and product. Clearly state that the life of your business is maintained by "word-of-mouth" referrals. Your client will appreciate that they were asked for referrals if they know that their friends, family, and neighbors are going to get good service. If you are asking for a referral in a letter, provide a stamped, self-addressed envelope for their convenience. Providing professional-quality materials for your client's referral will make you and your client look good. The *Contractor of Choice* is confident when asking for referrals.

Strategy #5

Pay a Referral Fee.

Reward your clients for their referrals. Create a thought-out referral fee program and let every one of your clients know about the program. Referral fees can take the form of cash, services, coupons, tickets to entertainment events, products, consultation, dinner vouchers, gift certificates, or anything else of value. The fee can be a flat fee or it can be a percentage of the new project price. In our design/build remodeling company in South Texas, we reward clients with a significant cash referral fee. When we secure a contract, we pay the client a fee and send another thank you letter reminding them that they can qualify for as many referral fees as they have friends. A referral fee encourages your client to market for you and promote you as the *Contractor of Choice*.

Strategy #6

Ask for a Referral as Part of the Sale.

This is a bold and useful promotion strategy. Many times a client will want to negotiate your prices. If you choose to discount your price, get something in return. Ask for referrals as part of the negotiation. Be smart about this. If you are able to secure at least three qualified, serious leads for new clients in exchange for negotiating your price, it may be worth some sort of discount. A referral to a qualified and serious new client can be included in the contract as part of your compensation. And when you end up working with these referred clients, remember to ask them for at least three referrals. With this strategy, you can see how your network of clients can grow very quickly.

Strategy #7

Have a "Talking Job Sign."

Post a 24-hour access phone number on your job sign. The phone number can be used to answer any questions that people passing by may have. You can answer the phone live or you can have a pre-recorded message about the project and your company. Include in the pre-recorded message interesting facts about the project where the sign was displayed. Include information that makes it easy to contact you for further discussion. Include your Website address.

Strategy #8

Brand Your Company.

Develop a unique way of identifying what you do. The terminology is important in this strategy. Make it short. Make it memorable. Make it clear and understandable. Your prospective customers should be able to clearly discern what your company is all about. The terminology you choose should be splashed on every piece of promotional material you have. A good way to start to brand your company is to ask your premier customers what they feel you do best. They know what your strongest attributes are and they will let you know. After asking several of your customers, a common theme will surface. From this theme, your brand will emerge. Test the terminology in the marketplace. Once you are certain of the fit, own it. For example, you might brand yourself as the *Contractor of Choice.* (Sound familiar?)

Strategy #9
Give Advice Away.

The laws of reciprocity say you will get back more than what you give away. As you gain knowledge and experience in your industry, be willing to share this with colleagues and new entrepreneurs. Share this willingly with potential customers, trade contractors, vendors, and employees. Give of your time, advice, and technical experience. The temptation is to hold on to any special knowledge you may possess. The reality is that when you share your advice and expertise, the pie doesn't get smaller, it actually grows. And a larger piece of the pie is what you want.

Strategy #10

Promote to Professional Services.

Promote your company as the *Contractor of Choice* to non-client influential professionals. Make your accountant, lawyer, broker, physician, and banker fully aware of all your services and products. You can also promote your company to association executives, insurance agents, politicians, and even your industry peers. Send your promotional materials to them regularly. Take them on a tour of a completed project. Offer them a discount when they use your product and service. They usually network with other professionals. Ask them for leads (see Strategy #4). These professionals may not need your services immediately, but eventually they will. By promoting your company to them regularly, these professionals will recommend you to their associates. One additional tip... If you are going to promote yourself to professionals, do so in the most professional manner possible.

Strategy #11

Introduce Your Staff.

The fact is that we tend to do business with people we like and who like us. A personal introduction of your key people can make your prospective client feel at ease. Let your client know that all of your employees are dedicated to serve. Often, a client just wants to know about the people who are doing the "hands on" work. Introductions can be made during personal visits to the prospective client's project site. Photographs and biographies of your employees can be included in your promotional material and on your company Website. Name badges can be worn by all of your employees to personalize their appearance to your customer's project site.

Strategy #12

Be Shameless.

Take great pride in shamelessly spreading the word about your business and the value it offers to others. Use every opportunity to proclaim yourself the *Contractor of Choice.* Some of the fanciest marketing programs in the world are no substitute for old-fashioned "shaking the bushes." Shameless promotion of yourself is an active process. Shameless promotion means planting seeds, adding value, responding, and setting up systems to draw people and opportunities to you. There is no excuse for not making the world aware of who you are and what you do. In case you have a bit of anxiety or fear about shamelessly promoting yourself, remember, "profits have a way of taking the fear out of promoting yourself."

Strategy #13

Call Your "Warm List."

The list of customers for whom you regularly work is your "warm list." This list of customers is warm to you and to your service. They are familiar with what you do. They are the greatest source of new business, since they already have an established relationship with you. Get on the phone and regularly call your current and past customers to ask if they need your services again. When calling, ask how they are benefiting from the service you have already performed for them, and ask for additional work. While you have them on the phone, ask for a referral lead of potential new customers. Calling customers from your "warm list" is much more profitable than cold-calling, and much less intimidating.

Power Tip

If you don't ask for what you want, that means you really don't want it. Start spreading the word today. The more you spread the word, the easier it gets!

— **Paul Montelongo**

Section 2

Print

Johannes Gutenberg's invention of the printing press in the mid-1400s is widely thought of as the origin of mass communication. The printing press marked Western culture's first viable method of disseminating ideas and information from a single source to a large and far-ranging audience. For centuries, the printed word has been used as an instrument to influence, educate, and promote. The advancement of technology has made it entirely possible for you to spread your printed message far and wide, and to do it with flair. There are literally thousands of ways to promote yourself as the *Contractor of Choice* with a printed message.

Why is printing so important? Any number of reasons comes to mind. First, it can be used to give clarity to your message. For example, you can explain all of your products and services with the right copy in a brochure. The printed message is also a visual aid. Many of your customers will process your message in a visual mode. When you can create visual images for them to remember, your message and your company impressions will be enduringly left on them. Your printed message can be plain, simple, and straight to the point. Your printed message can also be flamboyantly presented to your market with color, graphics, and logos that appeal to the eye. In all cases, test your printed marketing pieces before you invest a ton of money in the final product. The following *19 Power Strategies* will show you ways of using print that you may not have thought of to become the *Contractor of Choice*.

Strategy #14

Have a Great Business Card.

Your business card is a statement of your business credibility. Your business card should say who you are, what you do, and where you do it. Put your smiling face on the front of your card. People will remember your face. Put your list of services or your mission statement on the back. The business card is among the oldest marketing tools around. The card serves as a visual reminder of your business. A great business card will include an appropriate, descriptive, and memorable logo (see Strategy #30). The card will state the company name and a contact person's name and phone number. The card's design should be visually pleasing so your card is one your customers will remember. When you are having your business card designed, test market several of your designs with friends, customers, and strangers. Get a consensus on which design is most memorable. Every employee in your company should carry their own business cards. And remember to print your company Website (see Strategy #46) on your business card. This is critical, as it will lead your customer to your Website for much more information to let them know that you are the *Contractor of Choice*.

Strategy #15
Send Out a Newsletter.

Develop a monthly, quarterly, or even a semi-annual newsletter. Include the latest and most impressive news about your company. Include a suggestion, consumer tip, and free advice. Your company name and the visual layout are the two most important components of a newsletter design. A catchy title for your newsletter will make a greater impact on your customer. For example, a plumber may have a newsletter called *The Royal Flush* rather than *ABC Plumbing Company Newsletter*. An attractive layout will produce eye appeal and the memorable title will give you name retention. Include a customer-oriented publicity story. Insert photos of your projects. Make an offer your customer can respond to immediately. Say something unique about your business. A regularly sent newsletter will soon come to be expected by your customers.

Strategy #16
Have Lots of "Stuff."

"Stuff" in this context refers to all of the promotional material that you can create and gather to promote your company. Create brochures, one-page ads, and photographic promotional material to hand out at any time. Include in your material any awards and recognition you have received. Professionally reproduce any newspaper or magazine articles that have been written about your company. Do the same with the articles you have written and had published. Establish yourself as a professional contractor by having an appealing presentation folder. Include testimonial letters from satisfied customers in your promotional package. The *Contractor of Choice* always has lots of "stuff" to hand out.

Strategy #17

Label Your "Stuff."

Put your name and critical information on all of your "stuff." Let others know who you are and what qualifies you as the *Contractor of Choice.* Place your company logo and Website address on every piece of promotional material you have produced. Make it easy for customers to contact you. Label everything from your trucks and cars to your pens and pencils. If you must, have peel-off labels printed and stick them on everything that the public will see.

Strategy #18

Carry Your "Stuff."

Have your promotional material with you at all times. Carry your material to association meetings, networking social events, and business meetings. Be ready to hand them out at will. Keep your "stuff" updated and current. Put your "stuff" in a small carryall bag and take it with you everywhere you go. By the way, label your carryall bag, too.

Strategy #19

Have Free "Stuff."

People love small, usable, free things. Pens, pencils, notepads, mouse pads, coffee cups, business card holders, sticky notes, coasters, paper weights, and key chains are just a few. Carry these items with you at all times and give them away freely. Label every one of these with your company name and contact information. Give away free "stuff" to your prospective customers and to existing customers. How people appreciate these small items and remember where they came from is amazing. If you are able to give away a small sample of your product, this is an excellent way to promote yourself as the *Contractor of Choice*.

Strategy #20

Share Your "Stuff."

Leave your promotional materials with anyone who may be a source of new business. Vendor outlets and suppliers are an obvious place to start. You can set up a small display area at your vendors' locations and leave your promotional "stuff" for prospective customers to pick up. Create an alliance with your vendors and suppliers so they can do the same at your business location.

Strategy #21
Send a "Tip Sheet."

Send to people in your database (see Strategy #49 for tips on creating your database) a "tip sheet" from time to time. Give helpful tips on how best to use your service or product. The format for a "tip sheet" is simple. Briefly state a fact about your business. For example, an air-conditioning contractor may say, "Having a professional technician perform regularly scheduled maintenance on your home's central A/C unit is important. Here are the top ten reasons to have your unit checked regularly." Then proceed to list the top ten reasons and benefits to support your statement. This "tip sheet" can be a single sheet of paper in a tri-fold, mailed to the names in your database. Include a coupon or discount offer for some service you provide and a deadline date for the recipient to respond. Include all of your contact information and your company slogan.

Strategy #22

Send a "Special Report."

Got a new service or product? Send a "special report" to the names in your database. Design the report to look like the information is hot off of the press. In fact, state that the information you are sending is "new" or "results of a recent survey." Boldly stamp on the outside of the envelope, card, or tri-folded mailing that this is a "special report." Include in the report reasons to use your new product or service. People will usually open an envelope that is marked "special" or "special report" or even "confidential report."

Strategy #23
Send a Post Card.

Send thank you notes, post cards, and get well cards. This small courtesy shows concern and interest. Have your company name printed on the card. For a more personalized message, send a *Hallmark*™ card. Notice the conversations you have with people and pick up on what is important to them. Notice the events happening in their lives and with their business and send an appropriate greeting card. A word of encouragement sent at the right time can make a lasting impression.

Strategy #24
Send a Direct Mail Piece.

Direct mail allows you to take the most careful aim at your targeted customer. A direct-mail campaign can be extremely profitable when directed at the right segment of the population. The most critical element is sending the mail piece to the right list of prospects. This list can be arranged by virtually any demographic that you choose. Examine your existing customer profile. Where do they live or work? What is their average income? What time of year are they most likely to buy? Send a direct-mail piece that is a mirror reflection of the data you collect. You may also send a single colorful postcard with the question, "Did you receive the information I sent?" When they follow up with a phone call, you have made a new contact.

Strategy #25

Spruce Up Your Bulk Mail.

When mailing promotional pieces to prospective customers, send bulky envelopes and textured envelopes. They tend to be opened more frequently. Bulky envelopes generate curiosity. Also, hand-signed and hand-addressed envelopes are opened more frequently. Sprucing up your bulk mail in this way will increase your chance that prospective clients will open and read your mailing piece.

Strategy #26
Send Out Coupons.

Offer a discount coupon for your service or product. The coupon can be for a discount in service fees or can offer more service for the normal fee. Send these in your bulk mail-outs or as a separate mailing. A coupon can also be sent with your normal mail correspondence. Offer discounts in conjunction with your normal service. Make the discount worthwhile. Consider a regular coupon offer program. Your customers will begin to expect these and it will generate more business. You must ask for the additional business once you honor the coupon (see Strategy #3 - Ask, Ask, Ask).

Strategy #27

Have a Visually Appealing Job Sign.

Post your job signs all over the project. Make sure they are highly visible. A job sign is a great way to alert people to your business and a great way to remind them of your business. Place them on job sites and on the front wall of your office. If you have a project under construction at the corner of an intersection, place a sign facing each way so passersby will see the sign from every angle. Make your signs easy to read and state clearly how to contact you. Your signs should be legible, informative, non-cluttered, and clean. Invest in wood or press wood signs rather than plastic signs that are easily damaged.

Strategy #28

Place Your Brochure
On Your Job Sign.

Put your brochures, business card, and one-page advertising in a plastic container. Preferably, you will attach a water-resistant container for exterior use. Attach this container to your job sign for easy access. Include an information sheet about the project where the sign is placed. People are very curious and the more detailed the information, the more their curiosity will be satisfied. Include on your one-page advertising all of your contact information and a list of all of your services.

Strategy #29

T–shirt at the Theme Park.

I have actually seen this. Put a T-shirt on your kid and on yourself with your company logo when you go to the amusement park. If you have a company slogan, include this on the T-shirt. Put your Website on the T-shirt. People tend to remember that more easily than a telephone number. Sometimes you have to do something unexpected and different to promote your business. Who knows? You may get a lead and a sale.

Strategy #30
Have a Unique Logo.

Get a college student or graphic arts person to design a unique logo. A logo should be visually appealing and memorable. The logo should be an accurate reflection of your trade or business. I believe that it also must make a statement about your business philosophy. For example, if you wish to characterize your company as one that delivers speedy service, then a logo with lightening bolts and swooshing symbols might reflect that. Or, if you are a landscape company that wants to emphasize the plush green results of your lawn maintenance service, deep green blades of grass may be included in your logo. Make the logo fit your company profile. By the way, splash your logo on everything, including your kid's T-shirt (see Strategy #29).

Strategy #31

Put Your Picture on Your Truck.

This is a unique and memorable way to promote yourself. Doing this is not vain. This is a way for John Q. Public to put a face with a name. The picture identifies you as unique and gives a first impression to your client. Though a prospective customer might not need your service right now, the visual memory of your picture on your truck will get them thinking. The graphics on your vehicles should be easily distinguishable. They should be able to be read from at least 100 feet away.

Strategy #32
Take Lots of Photographs.

In our visually oriented society, a picture is indeed worth thousands of words. Project photos are most effective when there is a "before" and "after" photo. Also, keep photos of work-in-progress. Traditionally an 8" x 10" full color glossy is best for finished project photos. For "work-in-progress" photos and "before" photos, a 5" x 7" print will suffice. Make it easy for your customers to "see" what they are going to get. Your company portfolio should include photos of your most impressive projects and a few "normal" projects. Have photographs of your office and your fleet of trucks also. A photo of the principals of the company or of the company staff personalizes your business to prospective customers.

Power Tip

Promoting your company in print creates an historical record of your company. Customers will often save your printed material for years before they buy from you.

— Paul Montelongo

Section 3

Networking

Remember the Broadway show and movie *Six Degrees of Separation*? The title refers to the fact that there's a chain of no more than six people that links every person on this planet to every other person. In other words, if you want to meet the President of the United States and play golf with him, you know somebody who knows somebody (up to six people deep) who can make this meeting happen. More often than not, it doesn't take a chain of six people to create a meeting of this sort. That is, if your network is broad and deep. Networking is a way of connecting with people to find what you need and to provide to them what they need. Their networks become your networks as well. Networking is building relationships with people and organizations that can foster your professional and personal contacts. When you have an organized collection of personal and professional contacts, you are able to quickly find the person you need to get what you need in any given situation.

How do you know if you have a strong network? Take Harvey Mackay's 2 a.m. test. Mackay is the best selling author of the book *Dig Your Well Before You're Thirsty*. Mackay is a networking expert. He says that you must be able to build a network of contacts so strong and diverse that you can make a telephone call at 2 a.m. and get help. Having a medical crisis and need help at 2 a.m.? Call someone in your network. Stranded in an airport at 2 a.m.? Call someone in your network for help. These are contacts that you have developed, nurtured, and built a trusting relationship with over the years. The network could come in handy because as Mackay says, "2 a.m. is a lousy time to try to make new friends."

The following *13 Power Strategies* will help you know where you can build your network. As the *Contractor of Choice*, you must work within your industry to develop relationships. You certainly must go way outside the industry to broaden your network. You will also get a few ideas on what to do to make an impact in your network.

Strategy #33
Join Organizations and Associations.

Become an active member in the organizations that represent your specific segment of the construction industry. This will allow you an opportunity to rub elbows with key industry leaders. You will become known among your peers. By volunteering your services and assisting with committees, members come to know you personally. They then feel more comfortable in using your services or in referring your services to others. Join organizations and associations in your community that are not related to your industry, but that you can actively support. This is also a prime networking opportunity. Be prepared to "stay the course." Often, it takes time to get well connected in community associations. Don't bail out before your membership pays off.

Strategy #34

Represent Your Association.

Know the issues and take a stand for your industry. Reach out for a leadership position and speak on behalf of your industry association. Be selective with your speaking engagements. Speak to consumer groups and business organizations where potential clients gather. Give out valuable information about your industry trends, services, and the benefits of your association. Your involvement will give you credibility and will attract future business from those who hear you speak. Include any position that you hold in your association in your promotional material.

Strategy #35

Join "Lateral" Industry Associations.

Become active in the associations of the industries that support your contracting business. These include banking, real estate, insurance, material distributors, trade contractors, general contractors, etc. Your presence in these associations will give you direct contact with people who will give you business or send new business to you. Join these "lateral" industry associations with the purpose of promoting yourself as the *Contractor of Choice*. Branching out to these associations will broaden your customer base. Listen attentively to the needs of the members of these associations. You may see opportunities to create new services and products to fill their needs.

Strategy #36

Get on Boards of Directors in the Construction Industry.

Be a director for those organizations that promote the construction industry. In order to be on a board of directors, there is an implied commitment to your industry. Board appointments usually require that you have paid your dues in an organization with time and volunteer service. In return, you can accept appointments to Boards of Directors and use this opportunity to promote your company even more. Include your appointments to Boards of Directors in your promotional material. Send out a press release to the media and notices to the names in your database. This will add to your credibility in the community.

Strategy #37

Get on Boards of Directors of "Lateral" Industries.

A lateral industry or organization is that which supports your career industry. For example, bankers, mortgage lenders, and realtors frequently join contractor associations. Contractors, in turn, should join (and be active in) those industry associations that correlate to the construction industry. Being on the Boards of Directors of lateral industry associations offers an expanded opportunity to network and create new clients. The more people you know and the more people who know you increases your chances for new business.

Strategy #38

Join the Chamber of Commerce.

Join (and get involved in) the Chamber of Commerce in your city and in the area of the city in which your office is located. Attend the mixers, networking breakfasts, and trade shows. Carry your promotional material with you and spread the word about your company (see Section 1). In most cases, Chambers of Commerce encourage their members to do business primarily with other Chamber members. In most cities, the Chamber of Commerce has programs that specifically send visitors to do business with Chamber members. Your Chamber of Commerce will also likely have a business leads referral program.

Strategy # 39
Form Alliances.

You cannot increase your business alone. You must create alliances with other companies and individuals that can work in concert with you on your business ventures. Consider acting as a sub-contractor on larger projects in order to increase your expertise and get more project referrals. You may need to joint venture with others in your business to land bigger deals. Even the largest construction companies in the world will sub-contract or joint venture with other large companies to secure massive contracts. Look for opportunities to co-create projects or co-manage projects. Working in alliance groups tends to increase the size of projects you do without proportionally increasing the workload.

Strategy #40

Form a "Master Mind" Group.

In the classic personal development book, *Think and Grow Rich*, Napoleon Hill explains the importance of a Master Mind group. According to Hill, a "Master Mind" is defined as, "a coordination of knowledge and effort, in a spirit of harmony, between two or more people for the attainment of a definite purpose." Meet and regularly discuss business strategies with other successful contractors or entrepreneurs. Share your ideas, goals, and dreams with those who will support you. There is an enrichment of the thinking process when you associate with other successful entrepreneurs.

Strategy #41
Create a "Think Tank."

Similar to, but slightly different from a "Master Mind," a "Think Tank" usually involves concentrated discussions of the future. By getting involved with a forum of successful contractors, you can brainstorm the future of your industry, locally and as a whole. In general, a "Think Tank" answers the question, "What would happen if…?"

A "Think Tank" is a discussion based on imagining any possibility of the future with the members of your "Think Tank" group. This sort of brainstorming activity will generate enormous opportunities for your business. Being involved in a "Master Mind" or a "Think Tank" group truly endorses your commitment as the *Contractor of Choice.*

Strategy #42
Attend Industry Conferences.

Industry conferences provide an opportunity for you to compare your progress with other contractors and the industry as a whole. Learn what other contractors are doing to market and promote their services. Find out what is working and what is "hot" in the marketplace. When attending an industry conference, one can get overwhelmed with the ocean of information that is available. I suggest that you have a narrow focus when attending conferences. If you come away from the conference with just two or three specific strategies to help you continue your success, then the time and money you will have invested in the conference is worth it. Carry your "stuff" with you at these events and distribute them freely. Share your expertise and marketing ideas with others.

Strategy #43

Network, Network, Network.

Did I say network? Yes. Tell your friends and your enemies what you do and how it benefits people. Talk it up constantly. Even a company with little or no budget for marketing can make contacts with prospective clients. Visit with prospects at Chamber of Commerce meetings and at social functions. Be pleasant, professional, and have something good to say about what you do. The only cost associated with shaking hands and smiling at folks is the hours you spend doing this. Consider it an investment. Even companies with well-funded marketing budgets know the value of meeting and greeting people. In fact, they will pay employees to attend social functions to spread business cards and brochures. Networking (meeting and socializing at business functions), is a form of promotion that you should never stop. There is always someone that needs to know who you are and what you do. And there are people you need to know as well. Oh yes, did I mention networking?

Strategy #44

Develop a Top-25 Contact List.

Stay in constant contact with the top 25 people that can give you business immediately or that will refer you. I say top 25 because this seems to be a manageable number on a monthly basis. You may have more. These individuals know you best. They are your fans. They have hired you in the past and continue to hire you. Develop this list today. You may only start with five or ten. Even if it is only one person that you contact every 30 days, this list will grow as your business grows. If 25 is the number you choose to have, you will want to shuffle the list around from time to time. Remember these are the top 25 people that will send you the sort of client you want. Once a month, send them a card or make a phone call to them. Send them a post card while on vacation. Cut out a newspaper article and send it to them. Send them something of value. I occasionally will send out a credit card sized plastic card with motivational sayings. We all need to be inspired from time to time and these cards do just that. These cards can be found at www.gold-mind.com. The point is to have a consistent presence in front of these top 25 advocates of your business.

Strategy #45
Have a Trade Show Booth.

Your presence at trade shows indicates that you are serious about your business. Choose the shows that fit your company. Obtain a copy of the previous year's program guide to see if your booth would fit the show. Attend smaller shows first and move up to larger shows. Make sure your booth looks as good or better than the ones around you. The most successful trade show booths are the ones that stand out from the crowd. Successful booths have give-aways and some sort of interactive theme. Give people a reason to talk to you. Have a product to demonstrate, a model, or a contest. Post a thought-provoking question on your booth graphics. Make your booth interesting and informative. Have plenty of literature on hand and make it readily available for people to pick up. Network with other exhibitors to get more leads.

Power Tip

The broader and deeper your network of contacts, the greater chance you have to get what you want, when you want it.

— Paul Montelongo

Section 4

Electronic Technology

Technology is the tool that all *Contractors of Choice* must use fully. The Internet is a vehicle that will help you make more money and get the customers with whom you wish to work. Having your own Website is the great equalizer. A web presence makes the little guys look big. Anyone can position their company on the Internet in such a way to give a more expansive perception of their company.

John Henry, an architect in Orlando, Florida, says his dream is to build luxury homes all over the world. However, as an independent businessman taking personal care and oversight of each of his projects, he faced the challenge of marketing himself outside of his local area. That is, until the advent of the World Wide Web. Henry advertised his services on his Website. He had photos of luxury homes he had designed and that had been built. Every year, the highly rated morning television show Good Morning America has a program in which they showcase five exquisitely luxurious homes in America. The producer of Good Morning America performed a key word search for "luxury homes" on the Internet. Since Henry had a Website that featured photos of several of his projects, he got the call from the producer. Good Morning America featured a 14,000 square foot French Chateau that Henry designed. His Website is now permanently in the GMA Website archives. Anytime a visitor connects to the GMA Website they are able to travel in cyber space to John Henry's Website because they are linked. John is now designing and building "high-end" luxury homes in Florida, Texas, and California.

The following *11 Power Strategies* will help you get connected to technological concepts that will help you grow your business and become the *Contractor of Choice.*

Strategy #46

Have a Website.

Hellooooo! This is the new millennium. You must have an Internet presence. Compare this to having your own telephone number. You wouldn't even consider not having a telephone number. The Internet gives your customer 24-hour access to your business information. Your Website can be as interactive or as simple as you would like. In its simplest form, a Website is an on-line brochure to introduce your company to the world. More advanced sites offer products on-line and some can even host other Websites. You can get up and running with your own Website in a short period of time by putting your company information on Website templates or by creating your site with basic software programs. Whatever it takes you to get your company on the Internet, do it. A Website will give your company a whole new level of credibility. A company Website for the public to visit also saves you time and money. A visitor to your site will see your complete list of services and be familiar with your company prior to calling you. A Website is a way to pre-qualify potential customers.

Strategy #47
Link Your Website.

Affiliations with other contractors, vendors, trade contractors, and associations endorse the credibility of your business. Informational links are effective. Links to companies that serve your industry are effective. Link to manufacturers of the products you use most. Educate your customer on these products with links in your Website. Within your Website, link to media sources that have published material about your company. One strategy to have your Website listed at the top of search engines is to have many links in and out of your Website. Link popularity to your Website dictates the rating of your site in many search engines.

Strategy #48
Send an E-mail Newsletter.

Electronic magazines, or E-zines, allow you to send brief notes regularly by e-mail, with virtually no cost. These are sent to the names in your database with email addresses. There are several email programs on the market that will help you facilitate these E-zines. About 15 to 30 lines of text is all you need to capture the reader's attention. Offer some specific piece of information that is of value to your recipient. Write a "Top-10" list for your recipients. For example, "Here are the Top-10 reasons you should consider a professional design/ build company for your next renovation project."

Respect their privacy by offering an "opt-in" E-zine. In other words, give them the option to subscribe to your E-zine. Always have a link in your E-zine to your Website. Offer tips, coupons, discounts, specials, and reminders about your company. As with a paper newsletter, consistency is important. When offered regularly, an electronic newsletter pays.

Strategy #49
Create a Database.

A computerized database is a collection of information about customers and prospects. This type of database is more than a glorified mailing list. It includes, but is not limited to, name, phone number, address, email, prospecting records, sales records, purchase activity, and the best time to contact the prospect. There are several quality database software programs available on the market. Select one that allows you to customize your database to suit your needs. There is tremendous power in building your database. Virtually everyone you meet can qualify in some way to be a part of your database. A computerized database allows you the latitude to quickly send marketing information to your prospects and customers. When you have a new product, service, or a company announcement, you can almost immediately send information to your database. A quality database is a project that never ends. For as long as you own and operate your business, your database will continue to grow. This collection of information is one of the primary tools that you will use as the *Contractor of Choice.*

Strategy #50

Conduct On-line Training.

Technology now allows you to conduct training sessions over the Internet. This is an advanced method of Internet usage. Do this for your customers, personnel, potential customers, and the public. You can now offer simultaneous instruction on the telephone while your listener scrolls through their computer looking at instructional text or visual images. You can also place on your Website streaming video clips of your products or projects. An audio clip can be placed on your Website with information about your company. Technology will continue to advance. Being aware of the opportunities can set you apart from the crowd as the Internet savvy *Contractor of Choice.*

Strategy #51

Get In with Extranet Services.

Extranet services are those services used exclusively between businesses. "Business to business" alliances with vendors, suppliers, and customers via the Internet speed up transactions and reduce the time needed for normal paper transactions. Connecting your business to banking services and product manufacturers will give additional exposure to your business. Extranet services can be an entire community of contacts in themselves. This is the future of all business. With each Extranet service you subscribe to, include your company logo and as much promotional information as allowable.

Strategy #52

Send a "Web-card."

Send a post card with a full color replica of the home page of your Website. The visual association with your Website will invite prospective customers to visit your Website on the Internet. When you have a new product or service to unveil, do this through your Website and send a "web-card" simultaneously. Be sure to include on the "web-card" your Website address and your contact information. "Web-cards" can be sent to anyone in your database. They can be produced inexpensively and mailed to prospective customers. Carry additional "web-cards" with you to hand out at random or to include in your promotional packages. For more information visit www.web-cards.com or www.printing.com or call Color of Real Estate at 800-221-1220.

Strategy #53

Send a Mass Fax.

You know that database from Strategy #49? Another way to maximize its use is to send regular mass faxes to the names in your database. This is sometimes referred to as a broadcast fax. Be sure to comply with FCC guidelines on this. Once you comply, send notice of special discounts, current project information, or just a simple "thank you for your business."

Use your regular facsimile transmittal form as an opportunity to further promote your business. In a conspicuous location on your fax form, place an advertisement of an award your company has won or a reminder to call for new product and service updates.

Strategy #54

Promote with an Audiocassette Tape.

Record a 15-minute commercial of all the pertinent information about your company on an audiocassette tape. Say who you are, what you do, and who should call you. Include in the tape live testimonials from satisfied customers. You can also include referrals from your vendors and your banker. Give specific information on how a customer will benefit from your service. Educate your prospective client about how to buy your product or service. What steps should they go through to make a purchase? State your warranty information. Give a brief comment about the history of your company. Have an easy listening pace and tonality on the tape. You can have a local radio disc jockey put their voice on the tape for very little money, if any. Write the script and test market the script with some of your existing customers. Audiocassette tapes can be produced for under $2.00 each when you have several hundred done at one time.

Choice #55

Get a Toll Free Number.

An 800 telephone number is a low cost way for customers to be encouraged to call you. With the proliferation of toll free numbers, the phone company now offers 866, 877, and 888 numbers. Toll free numbers are very inexpensive and they eliminate the barrier of a long distance charge. Even if your primary market area is only local, an advertised toll free telephone number can give the public the perception that your business is large. Place your toll free phone number on all of your promotional material.

Strategy # 56
"On-hold" Promotion.

Record a message that promotes your company to callers on hold. This can be a repeating audiocassette tape or a compact disc. Talk about your services and your awards. Give recognition to your employees and mention them by name. This personal touch introduces your employees to the caller. The message should include any special offers, discounts, increase in services, or new products that your company offers. Thank the caller for their patience and mention that you will give them your undivided attention when you return.

Power Tip

In business, as in life, a small distinction can make all the difference in your success. Your understanding of the power of technology can explode your business to new creative heights.

— Paul Montelongo

Section 5

Media
Promotion

In the spring of 1979, two entrepreneurial executives of a very small residential remodeling firm in San Antonio held a brainstorm session with a local advertising executive. The remodeling firm was relatively new in business, only four years old. The firm had enjoyed a small measure of success, and was gaining a reputation for quality work, fair prices, and great customer service. The specific issue being discussed was how to propel the business into the limelight. What advertising strategies would put this company on the map? What promotional tactics would allow this small remodeling firm to dominate the local market with an awareness of its product and services? In the uncertainty, one thing was sure, it had to be big.

The world champion Dallas Cowboys football team provided the answer. A player from "America's Team," as they were affectionately known, would play a role in the growth of this small remodeling company. The player to endorse this company was none other than all-pro free safety Charlie Waters. Waters had been voted "Most Popular Cowboy" the year before and he was greatly admired in Texas for his athletic prowess and hard-nosed, yet class act style of play. The executives decided that Waters was the answer and they would pursue his services. Now, remember this was in 1979, when endorsements from professional athletes was a fledgling business. Several months passed with little progress. Then in the pre-season of 1979, Waters was injured and had to sit out the remainder of the season. He was now available for endorsement services.

In a flurry of action, Waters was contacted, accepted the offer, visited the remodeling firm's office and inspected several projects. Waters decided that he could endorse the remodeling firm. In one day, Waters filmed two television commercials. To his credit, he was as much a professional on the filming set as he was on the football field. The advertising campaign would be a huge success that created the brand, "Go With the Pro." Though the investment was heavy at the time, approximately $10,000 in production and talent cost, the pay-off was huge. The chief executive of this meeting, Armando had taken a chance. He had seen the future and seized the opportunity. Armando realized that the power of the media is incredible. When your company is in the news and takes advantage of the press, the public attaches a great deal of credibility to your company.

Armando's vision can be your vision. The power of the media is enormous if you know how to work with it and see its benefits. There are many more options now than in 1979. The media and media resources can play an instrumental role in the success of your company. The following 7 *Power Strategies* will help you explore many of the media opportunities available. Many of these strategies can be used immediately. Others will take time to develop. Some are very low cost and others may mean more of an investment of your time and capital. Weigh the benefits and get in the game to become the *Contractor of Choice.*

Strategy #57

Send Out Press Releases.

You can submit a news release to newspapers and radio at no cost and receive free publicity. Any bit of good news that your company has should become public knowledge. Notify the press of promotions within your company, hiring of new personnel, contract awards received, office relocation or expansion, results of surveys you have completed, and expansion of your services. Also, send press releases to trade journals and association newsletters. Your press release needs to be brief, direct, and specific. Sending a good photograph never hurts. Once your news release is submitted, you will know when it has hit the press. Your customers, friends, and family will be calling. Keep press clippings in your promotional material.

Strategy #58
Contribute Articles.

Write an article on a hot topic in your trade or industry. Write a "do-it-yourself" or a "don't-do-it-yourself" article for the local newspaper. Write an article about the top 10 mistakes people make when selecting a contractor. Donate this to the local newspaper and your association newsletter. They are always looking for new material. Include at the end of the article a brief biographical history of yourself and your company. Include in the bio a line or two from your "elevator speech" that specifically describes what your company does for its customers (see Strategy #2). If you have reservations about your wordsmith abilities, have someone else write down your thoughts in a logical, coherent manner. Published articles identify you as an expert in your industry.

Strategy #59

Be a Television or Radio Guest.

Let the local media know that you are an expert in your trade or industry. Let them know that you are available to answer any consumer questions they have. Be ready to respond to them immediately. Stay aware of current topics in the news and identify how your business is related to that topic. If, in any way, you offer solutions to a problem in society, notify your local media and offer to be interviewed. When being interviewed by the media, keep your answers and comments brief and to the point. The media generally is looking for "sound bites" and will edit any long-winded comments.

Strategy #60
Write a Book.

The quickest way to become an acknowledged expert in your field is to be published. Experts get business. You likely have experiences in your business that are unique to you only. Write about these experiences. If you have obtained special training or practical knowledge that will help other contractors, write about it. If you have material that will benefit the public, write about that. Americans are thirsty for knowledge. When you write a book, it endorses you as an expert in your field and in your industry. At first, you may want to write a small "how-to" book. Even this kind of book gives you enormous credibility. When your prospective customer asks you what you do, imagine the impact in handing them a book that you have authored.

Strategy #61
Write a Chapter for a Book.

So, you say you don't have time to write a book? Though it is no easy task, there is another way. Write a chapter for someone else's book. You can collaborate with other industry professionals to write a book about a specific need in the marketplace. You get almost the same impact as writing the entire book yourself. You will contribute to the book as a recognized expert. Experts get business.

Strategy #62

Be Quoted and Quotable.

Get quoted in newspapers, magazines, newsletters, and trade journals. Be available and have something short, valuable, and memorable to say. Any time your name is mentioned, it adds credibility to your business. As with being interviewed on television or the radio (see Strategy #59), being quoted is only as good as the timeliness of your quote. Stay informed with local community needs and issues. Make your comments appropriate to those issues. Keep copies of your quotes and put them in your promotional material.

Strategy #63
Read and Write.

After reading an article from a trade journal, write the author and express interest in the article. Share your views and support. Magazine and newspaper editors love to receive responses from their readers. And the interesting thing is that the more controversial your comment, the more likely it is to be printed. Even if you disagree with an author's position, you can express yourself in a way that challenges readers to think about your point of view. Ask to be interviewed. This may show up in future articles, making you a recognized expert.

Power Tip

You must be fearless and relentless to capitalize on media promotion. Media promotion takes real commitment. The rewards far outweigh the risks.

— **Paul Montelongo**

Section 6

Community
Commitment

Terry Richardson has two grandsons playing Little League baseball in Momence, Illinois. Momence is a small town just outside Chicago with a population of approximately 3,000. Terry's grandsons were playing baseball all over town, literally. They had no regular field at which to practice and play games. Practice and games were moved from school to school and were subject to availability. Terry knew that there had to be some way to build a ball field with the town's limited resources. Terry owns a fencing company in Chicago and primarily works in the inner city area with his fence-building products and services.

Terry initially had some reservations about tackling the project of building a baseball field. Like many people, he originally thought the whole project might end up being done by him and his crews only. However, with a little faith in the small community of Momence, Terry mobilized the community to build the Little League field for his grandsons and their teammates. Members of the community came together and volunteered their time, money, energy, and expertise to get the ball field built for the kids. Terry sought help from his fence suppliers and one of them donated much of the fencing material. Other parents donated roofing material, building material, and equipment. Many parents and residents of the community donated their precious weekend time to labor for the Little Leaguers. Even the mayor of Momence got involved to help build the ball field.

Over a five-weekend stretch of time, a beautiful new Little League ball field was built, complete with a large backstop, six-foot perimeter fence, and dugouts covered by a shingled roof. Terry Richardson says that he just coordinated the effort and provided some technical support for the project. However, Terry's commitment to his grandsons and to their community was the motivating force behind the ballfield project. The following *9 Power Strategies* will suggest ways for you to make a commitment to help your community. This is a key component to becoming the *Contractor of Choice*.

Strategy #64
Community Involvement.

Contribute your experience, time, and resources to a community project. Volunteering is a great way to get enormous personal satisfaction from your career. Each of you reading this book has the capacity and expertise to volunteer your time and resources in some fashion to create a better society. Community involvement keeps you in touch with the real challenges of our society and can make you think of solutions. Solutions are the key to any successful business. When you offer solutions to your clients, your employees, your vendors, and your community, there is no ceiling on your success. The awareness of creating solutions on every level of your life will enhance your business and will definitely make you the *Contractor of Choice.*

Strategy #65
Teach a Class.

Continuing education classes for school districts and local colleges provide an opportunity to show what you know. Adult education courses are an ideal way to find customers. Obtain a copy of the adult education schedules from community education centers. See what types of classes they offer, and prepare a class related to your profession. Then approach the person in charge and ask to teach the course. Most of the time there is a small salary included for your efforts. The greater pay-off is that there is a good chance to meet prospective customers. Be sure to post the description and location of any class you teach in a visible location in your business. Teaching a class helps your credibility, and it lets customers know your level of commitment to your industry and to the community.

Strategy #66

Include Your Company in a Job Fair.

Job fairs take place frequently in your community and are an excellent opportunity to showcase your company. They can be a prime occasion to network with other business people. Large companies, civic groups, or Chambers of Commerce usually sponsor job fairs. Prospective employees look for good companies at job fairs. A job fair is generally a high visibility event. Local radio and television stations usually promote job fairs on the air. Make sure your company name is included in the advertising for the job fair. Have plenty of your promotional material at your booth and pass it out generously.

Strategy #67

Be a Business Coach.

A business coach is someone who guides, directs, and trains other entrepreneurs. The coach also sets out goals for the client and holds them accountable for their progress. A coach has practical experience that they are willing to share. A Professional Business Coach will customize the instruction to suit the needs of the client. Coach a young entrepreneur. Coach a new businessperson. Share your knowledge. They will show gratitude by telling others what a great person you are. Get involved in mentor programs as well. Mentors typically teach by example and monitor the progress of their mentees.

Strategy #68
Be a "Title" Sponsor.

Be a "title" sponsor for the Little League, Pop Warner, Youth Soccer League, Theatre Arts, Booster Clubs, Fundraisers, Golf Tournaments, Luncheons, etc. A title sponsorship is exactly as it is named. Your company name is splashed all over the event that you are sponsoring. The size of the event dictates the amount of money you will lay out for the sponsorship. In cases where there is a large sum of money, you can get your trade contractors and vendors to co-sponsor the event. Publicity for you will also benefit those with whom you do business. You can also consider an alliance with several contractors to be the "title" sponsor of an event.

Strategy #69
Get a Sponsorship.

Is there an organization or community group that you feel is a worthy cause? Ask for other companies and organizations to sponsor an effort you support. Put together co-operative money to sponsor some event. Your local builder's association or contractor group can collectively sponsor a Youth Sports League or a "Clean up the Neighborhood Day." Give credit to the association and give your company credit. Keep press clippings of these events and take photos to include in your promotional material.

Strategy #70

Support Consumer Groups.

Consumer groups come in many forms. Primarily, they represent segments of the community that need financial, legal, or public representation. Typically, their agenda is to defend the rights and privileges of consumers. To make a meaningful contribution to these groups is a promotional strategy that pays handsomely with good public relations. Offer your expertise, time, or cash to support those groups that support your community. There tends to be a higher level of publicity with the media concerning consumer groups. The ultimate position in this promotional strategy is to be the leader of a consumer group with a worthy cause.

Strategy #71

Have Your Own Seminar.

Conduct a seminar in which you teach "how-to" techniques. Also, teach "why-should." "Mr. customer, this is why you should choose a reputable contractor." These seminars can be held at your place of business, in the conference room of a local hotel, or at a meeting facility. Offer door prizes to your guests. Have plenty of your "stuff" for them to take away (see Strategy #16). These types of seminars must have lots of valuable content to justify your guest's investment of time and energy. Offer solutions to common problems experienced by your customers. For example, a landscape contractor can offer tips and techniques to help the public conserve water by xeroscaping their lawn. Then offer your service or product as a natural solution to the challenges you have presented in the seminar.

Strategy #72

Have Sweepstakes or a Contest.

Contests and sweepstakes attract people. Entrants become involved with you and involvement can lead to sales. The primary purpose of contests and sweepstakes is to get names to add to your database. They also separate you from your competition. Offer something that your primary customer will use and be to their benefit. Offer consolation prizes in order to maintain good rapport with entrants. Check with your legal advisor to get the rules of the contest to conform to local laws. Follow up with additional offers of value. Announce and publicize the names of the winners, the prize received, and your company as the sponsor of the contest.

Power Tip

Your legacy will not be measured by what you have acquired. Rather, history will note how you "showed up," who you were, and what you contributed.

—Paul Montelongo

Section 7

Recognition and Praise

The Vince Lombardi trophy. The Pulitzer Prize. The Stanley Cup. The Nobel Prize. The Emmys and Oscars. The Green Jacket. What do these all have in common? They are symbols of victory and achievement. They are outward visible testimonials of one's accomplishments on the field, in literature, on the ice, around the links, and on the stage. The holders of these symbols will forever be able to say that at one time, in one place, and for one segment in history, they were the best in the business.

To receive praise and recognition for one's accomplishments is an essential ingredient of the human makeup. Everyone needs to know that they are accepted and acknowledged for their hard work.

Contractors are not any different. You need commendation too. If you are going to receive praise, then strategically use it to promote yourself as the *Contractor of Choice*. Give yourself a competitive advantage by searching for ways to be professionally recognized. Most everyone I know likes a winner. Your customers will be impressed if you are a winner. The following *5 Power Strategies* will give you some ideas for getting noticed. Once you are noticed, use it to market yourself.

Strategy # 73

Win Awards.

Nominate yourself for all sorts of awards, and then win them. You will be surprised how many awards companies nominate themselves to win. There are awards to be won in your local association, in the Chamber of Commerce, and from state and national associations. Newspapers frequently award business professionals. Charitable organizations often give away Business of the Year awards. The amount of awards you can win is limitless. Proudly use your awards as promotional tools. Include your awards in all of your promotional material. Take photos of you accepting the award and submit the photo to the business review section of your local newspaper. The public is impressed with award winners.

Strategy #74
Get testimonials.

Obtain testimonials and reference letters from your satisfied customers. In order to save time and energy, write the rough draft of the letter yourself, if you must. Ask your customer to transfer it to their stationary and then have them sign it for you. A testimonial letter should contain a specific benefit or area of satisfaction that your customer has experienced. For example, "I appreciate the way our project was kept clean. I am most pleased with the fact that our project was done on time and on budget." Attach the testimonial letter to a photograph of the project. Put these letters in your "stuff" (see Strategy #16).

Strategy #75

Get Customer Evaluation Forms.

Design an evaluation form that is easy for your customers to complete. This can be as simple as a post card with five to ten questions about your service and product. Have your customers return an evaluation form to a neutral third party location. They will be more apt to give an honest opinion of your business. Collect the evaluation forms and use them to improve your business. Send a thank you note and a small gift to those customers taking the time to complete an evaluation form. If you have the evaluation form sent to a third party neutral location, send the thank you note from that same location. An evaluation form from your customers is critical. The only way to improve your business is to ask your customer what works and what needs to work better.

Strategy #76

Ask Directly for Customer Feedback.

Conduct an in-person interview or a telephone interview with your customers. Ask directly for their feedback. When you ask directly, they will usually tell you. Ask about the service, the product, timeliness in delivery, and professionalism of your staff. Directly ask what drew them to your company. What source of advertising did they notice that prompted them to call your company? Ask them to discuss your good characteristics and to candidly discuss needed areas for improvement. Knowing what your customers say about your strongest quality is important. That knowledge will help you to promote yourself better to potential new customers. Listen carefully to what your customer is saying, and to what they do not say. A vocal customer can be a blessing in disguise.

Strategy #77
Advertise in Strange Places.

Ads on bus benches, taxicab marquis, grocery store receipts, theatre screens, bumper stickers, and coupons can be effective. Advertising in strange and unique places can have somewhat of a disarming effect. The thinking here is that something different can "shake the bushes," so to speak. There are customers everywhere. Your customers shop, play, and socialize in many of the same places you do. Look for opportunities to advertise your business where people congregate. An unconventional approach in your marketing plan can bring in new customers.

Power Tip

Everyone likes a pat on the back for work done well. The greatest rewards in life are the ones on the other side of what is difficult and challenging.

— Paul Montelongo

Section 8

The
Psychology
of Selling

The psychology and mental awareness of marketing and promoting your business is very important. The psychology of selling your product or service is of even more importance. In order to give yourself the competitive edge and to market your company in the most effective way, you must master the art of selling. The promotional and marketing strategies presented in this book so far will only help you "get your foot in the door." The *Power Strategies* in this book will only encourage your customers to make the initial call to your office requesting a brochure, some additional information, or asking you to furnish a bid for a proposed project. You and you alone, must *sell* your product or service. You must get the prospective customer to sign their name on your contract and agree to pay your price.

There are thousands of sales technique courses and seminars available. Each of them teaches many of the same principles. I conduct educational sales seminars myself. There is one thing about all of them. Selling is a mindset. Selling is an inner game. What is going on in the mind of a salesperson makes all the difference in his/her success. This selling mindset is a psychology that involves constant improvement and practice. Some folks are natural born salespeople. You and I both know that. They are in the minority. For the rest of us, selling is a learned art, an educational process that must be rehearsed day after day.

The following *14 Power Strategies* relate mostly to *selling* your product. There are some interesting twists to some of the tactics to which you may have become accustomed. The marriage between marketing and selling your services will be the determining factor in your success. Use these strategies to become the *Contractor of Choice*.

Strategy #78

Refer to Your Price as an "Investment."

The price of your service or product can be referred to in many ways. You can say price, quote, charge, fee, cost, estimate, tab, bill, expense, or many others. As the *Contractor of Choice,* consider your price as an "investment" or an "investment opportunity." This change in your terminology alone will reap huge rewards. Especially when your product or service is a high investment item, you should use this phrase. When you perform services to a residence or a commercial property, your work is an investment to the owner. Also, rather than receiving draws on your contract, design your paperwork to say you are receiving investment disbursements.

The psychology of selling your services dictates that you give your potential buyer every possible reason to buy from you. One of the most common objections in the construction business (and most other businesses, in fact) is, "It costs too much. I can't afford it."

By referring to your price as an "investment" from the beginning of your negotiations, you begin to break down this common objection from the start. Consider the possibility that your prospective client is really saying, "Please show me how I can afford this."

Strategy #79
Offer "No Discount."

Sometimes the certainty of a firm, non-negotiable price is very attractive. When you present your price as firm and with no "wiggle" room, the buyer wonders what is so special that a discount won't apply. They must find out. Make your proposal clear and state all of the benefits and services you intend to furnish. Make sure you deliver. This strategy is very powerful. Many contractors will not budge on their price. I applaud this, because they know exactly what they want financially and know they can deliver the goods.

This strategy is supported by a long list of benefits you intend to furnish to your customer. Your entire sales presentation should revolve around the benefits your customer will receive when they contract with you to perform their project. You should rarely or never discuss the benefits to you personally, financially, or otherwise. In virtually every case, your prospective customer is interested in one thing and one thing only: "What is in it for me?" Silently, and even unconsciously, prospective customers are asking themselves this question every time you speak. So, answer it aloud with benefit after benefit after benefit.

How do you know what benefits to emphasize? Become a professional listener. The more you listen, the more your customer will talk. The more they talk, the more they will share what it is they really want from you or from a contractor. Ask leading questions to elicit more information from your customer. An example of a leading question could be, "Mrs. Jones, what else do you plan to do with your new room addition?"

Learn to ask review questions also. You might say to Mrs. Jones, "So, what I understand from our conversation is that you want to have a special environment for your family to get together. Is that right Mrs. Jones?" And then listen intently for the answer and any supplemental information.

If you are going to offer a "no-discount" or "non-negotiable" investment schedule for your services, you need to have the total confidence of your customer. You can do this by building unbreakable rapport with them during the sales investigation period. Asking questions and listening, listening, listening is the most powerful way to accomplish this.

Strategy #80
Send a "Draft" Proposal.

Contractors submit multiple proposals before a final agreement with an owner is reached. Stamp "draft copy" on the front of your initial proposals. This tells the client that you are willing to work with them through the buying and decision-making process. A draft copy also sets their mind at ease and lets them know that they can enter negotiations with you and have some hope that you will work out a deal with them. Presenting a proposal in this way also allows you to alter your proposal as you learn more about the prospective customer's needs, desires, and budget. A "draft copy" rubber stamp is a valuable tool to get more business.

Strategy #81

Be Dedicated to Serve.

Your customer will easily detect an attitude of service. Dedication to excellent service is a mindset more than anything else. Include in your company mission statement your willingness to serve your customers. When customers know your mission is to serve their best interests, they will beat a path to your door. The attitude of service is contagious. Your employees, vendors, and trade contractors will adopt this attitude as well. You can include your commitment to service in your "elevator speech" (see Strategy #2) and in all of your "stuff" (see Strategy #16). An attitude of service can be woven throughout all of your marketing plans. When the competition is tight, the company who offers the most competent service, the most personal interest, and the greatest commitment to professionalism will win.

Strategy #82

Be Responsive.

Your quick response to telephone calls, letters, and e-mails is appreciated by others. Your response is a reflection of the way you do business. Offer a guaranteed response time with your service. A plumbing contractor in San Antonio guarantees that a service vehicle will respond within one hour of the initial telephone call. All of this company's advertising states this guarantee. Be extra responsive to any warranty issues or challenges with your projects. Responsiveness is a predominant trait for the *Contractor of Choice*.

Strategy #83

Empower Your Employees.

Encourage your employees to brag on you as the *Contractor of Choice*. Give your employees total permission to promote your company. Help them to appreciate the value of powerful marketing and promotion. Discuss new promotional ideas with them and get their feedback. Explain your marketing strategies to them so that they feel involved in the process. Give permission to your vendors and trade contractors to boast about your company as well. Reassure your employees, vendors, and trade contractors that when everyone promotes your company, everyone earns more money.

Strategy #84

Offer Employee Incentives.

Offer incentives and bonuses to your employees when they create a new client. Offer incentives to them for a new idea that brings in new clients. Offer cash rewards for employees with money saving, moneymaking, or timesaving ideas. This will demonstrate your interest in their input and encourage them to continue to offer help. Encourage your employees to get involved in the promotion of your company at all levels. Help them to understand that promotion is a never-ending commitment and the more they are involved, the more money they will earn.

Strategy #85

Lead by Example.

Create a purpose for your marketing plan and share it with your organization. Maintain an optimistic view of your promotional plan. Stick to your purpose and your plan. Enthusiastically pursue new business at every opportunity. Be ready, willing, and able to do the little things to promote your business. "Walk the talk" and be willing to ask other people how you are doing. Listen to their response with an open mind. When your employees and trade contractors see you promoting yourself vigorously as the *Contractor of Choice*, it will be easier for them to do the same. The bottom line is that success in your company starts with you.

Strategy #86
Be Professional.

Be the sort of contractor with whom you would want to do business. Dress, act, and speak as the professional contractor you are. A basic rule of thumb is… Dress one level better than your competition. Speak with a positive voice. Phrase your words in a way that encourages those with whom you do business. Use vocabulary that is familiar to your customer. Avoid the jargon of the construction industry with your customer unless you are certain they understand the technical language. Act with professional conduct. Keep your office, equipment, and vehicles clean and professional looking. Years ago, I attended a seminar that spent thirty minutes teaching the participants how to shake hands like a professional. At the time, I remember thinking, "This is silly. I was taught this by my parents." However, I still remember that seminar decades later. And there were people at the seminar hearing the handshake information for the first time.

Strategy #87

Be Creative.

Got an idea that is different from those in this book? Do it, and do it well. Uniqueness is a very attractive quality. The only limit that you have is the limit of your imagination. With technological advances the way they are, there is every reason to believe that your creativity will be rewarded. Take a few minutes in each day to contemplate and imagine what could be possible with your marketing and promotion plan if you would just allow yourself to be creative. Ask yourself, "What else can I do to promote myself as the *Contractor of Choice?*" After arriving at that answer, ask again, "What else can I do?" Continually asking this sort of question keeps your mind open for all kinds of creative marketing schemes.

Strategy #88
Send a "Thank You" Note.

What a concept! The *Contractor of Choice* does this regularly. A simple thank you note can work wonders for good customer relations. Always remember to verbally say "thank you" and then follow up with a note card. It seems like such a simple thing to remember. However, as you get busy in the day-to-day activities of running your business, it is easy to forget. Make a conscious effort to say thank you and turn it into a habit. This simple strategy is the least expensive piece of advice you will ever receive, yet will yield the greatest results.

Strategy # 89

Remember the "Golden Rule."

This is another piece of advice that the *Contractor of Choice* always remembers. In fact, this should be a guiding principle in your business. Treating others as you would like to be treated is a fundamental approach to a successful business and a successful life. Applying this principle alone will save you more time and energy than you can imagine. It will open opportunities for new business and keep your existing customers happy and calling back to do more business with you. Remembering the "Golden Rule" will allow you to spend more time driving to the bank to make deposits instead of sitting in a lawyer's office giving depositions. And most important, treating others as you would like to be treated is the right thing to do.

Strategy #90

Be Fearless.

Fear of rejection or embarrassment can immobilize a person. There are two types of people...those watching the game and those playing the game. Get in the game with all you have. Stretch yourself to be the best you can. Many marketing and promotion tactics leave the control of the contact to the customer. The *Contractor of Choice* takes charge by using strategies that take their product to the customer. There is a strange phenomenon about overcoming fear. The more you do the thing you fear, the easier it becomes. And the results of fearless promotion are increased profits. Somehow, profits tend to help you overcome fear as well.

Strategy #91

Keep Score.

Keep score on what works and what does not work. Another way to say this is to measure your progress. Knowing the impact of your promotional dollar is important. Spend more time, money, and resources on what works to become the *Contractor of Choice*. Evaluate your progress on a monthly, quarterly, semi-annual, and annual basis. Another good exercise is to reflect on where you were three years ago, five years ago, or even ten years ago. This assessment of your progress will give you a reality check. Also, set up goals and benchmarks for upcoming years. When you reach those points in time, check the score again. Knowing where you are at all times with your promotional results is a huge key to success.

Power Tip

The creativity and sharpness of your mind is the greatest weapon you possess. From your mind comes all prospects for the future, and every sort of solution and success imaginable.

— Paul Montelongo

Section 9

Commitment
to Excellence

The Olympic record for the men's high jump event is 7'10". Set in 1996 at the Atlanta Games, this unbelievable achievement is an example of a commitment to excellence. The record is an example of excellence in one sport by a variety of competitors over many years of training. In 1960, the men's Olympic high jump record was a mere 7'1". Over a 36-year time frame, the record was improved by only nine inches. Thirty-six years of training, commitment, planning, and practice resulted in a small incremental improvement in the overall record. Each time the bar was raised and each time a new height became the record, it represented a commitment to excellence. An interesting fact about this achievement is that not every Olympic Games could boast of a new high jump record.

A commitment to excellence is an ongoing process. Commitment is a series of steps, an attitude that makes you take an honest look at where you are in your business today and ask yourself what needs to be corrected, and then fix it. A commitment to excellence is the embodiment of the phrase, "If it ain't broke, break it," then make it better.

Your commitment to excellence requires that you set lofty goals and you work to achieve those goals. The following *10 Power Strategies* will challenge you to look at your commitment to becoming the *Contractor of Choice*.

Strategy #92

Invest in Yourself.

Read, study, and attend seminars that build your professional and personal knowledge base. Develop a library of books, tapes, videos, and CDs that will advance your journey to greater success. There is no substitute for being a life-long student of business. It has been said that when a person fails to grow, they die. They die intellectually, morally, spiritually, and physically. The same is true in business. With rapidly changing technology and the advancement of better products, contractors must stay informed. Education may cost money, but lack of education costs much more. The best investment you can make is in yourself.

Strategy #93

Get a Coach.

Most professional athletes and entertainers have a personal coach. There are voice coaches, strength coaches, nutrition coaches, image coaches, etc. There is a distinct advantage to having customized personal training. Having someone hold you accountable to your goals and plans is invaluable. Take advantage of the services of a Professional Business Coach only if you have dreams of success bigger than most individuals. A Professional Business Coach will nurture you, encourage you, challenge you, and celebrate your success with you. Your Professional Business Coach will show you how to select a goal and achieve it. Your Coach will endorse you as someone who is worthy of the trust of others. If your goal is to become the *Contractor of Choice*, a Professional Business Coach is a wise investment.

Strategy #94
Turn it Upside Down.

I have read that the definition of insanity is when a person expects different results as they continue to use the same wrong action again and again. If your marketing and promotion plan is not creating the results you desire, *stop the insanity.* If you want different results, do something different. If you want to be more profitable, or if you want a better quality of clientele, do something different. Take a chance and approach your marketing plan from a different angle. Do the unthinkable. Do something unexpected. Do something extraordinary. Extraordinary people get extraordinary results.

Strategy #95
Follow Up.

The best leads and contacts in the world are only as good as the follow-up work you do. Sure it takes work, but it is worth it. With all of this promotional and marketing work you will be doing now, the leads will pour into your office. Create a systematic approach to handle the leads. Make immediate contact with potential clients as they call in to your office. Send an immediate thank you note for their business and respond to them promptly in some way. The normal sales cycle in our economy for large ticket items can take more than twelve months. When the call comes in to do business, follow up right away. This will uniquely qualify you as the *Contractor of Choice.*

Strategy #96

Be Persistent.

There is no substitute for hard work and persistence. If you don't take care of your customers, someone else will. Going out and finding customers is especially important when customers have a long contemplation period. You must maintain a constant presence in front of prospective customers. When the buying cycle is prolonged, the greatest advantage you have is persistence. Persist in your promotional strategies, your networking, and your follow-up activities. When the time is right for your prospect to buy, they will remember you as the *Contractor of Choice*.

Strategy #97

Decide to Make a Difference.

The original Latin word for decide, in essence, means to cut off all possibilities of failure. In other words, when you make a decision to do something and you have the resolve to accomplish a thing, you cannot help but succeed. Staying in the construction business and promoting yourself as the *Contractor of Choice* requires a decision on your part. Deciding to make a difference and a valuable contribution to the construction industry will give you a sense of purpose. The *Contractor of Choice* works from a sense of purpose. When you have a sense of purpose of activity, you will be able to implement the strategies contained in this book. From that sense of purpose, you will decide to be the *Contractor of Choice*. Deciding to make a difference in your business and in the lives of your customers and employees will drive you to succeed beyond your wildest imagination. Decide now. Decide to make a difference.

Strategy # 98

Create a Promotional Plan.

A promotional strategy calls for a well-balanced way to communicate regularly with your customers and prospects. Look at your promotional plan for the next 12 months. Then break it down into one-month increments. In other words, determine which specific strategies you will use each month. Likely, you will use one, two, or three strategies on a regular basis. For example, you may mail out a newsletter four times a year. You may host an educational seminar twice a year and you may attend a trade show once a year. If these are your primary promotional strategies, start to build your annual plan around these. Plan for one or two specific strategies that you will use every month. These may include sending a post card to your existing client database and working on the Board of Directors of an industry association.

Next, plan to implement one or two new strategies over the next twelve months. For example, you may want to write articles for a local newspaper or industry newsletter. It may take the better part of the year for you to write and edit the articles, make the right editorial contacts, and then have them published. This writing strategy, once implemented, could become one of your primary strategies in the following year.

The point is that you must have a plan. If you fail to plan, you are planning to fail. If you don't have a promotional plan in place right now, start. Don't leave the marketing and promotion of your company to chance. I think sometimes small business owners put off the marketing plan for fear that it may not work or that it may be too expensive. As you have seen in this book, there are dozens of low-cost and no-cost ways to promote your company. As one strategy works, leave it in your plan and make it better. If one is not as effective over time, replace it with another strategy.

You are your best resource for marketing and promotion. Start today and the results will be very rewarding. Take a few minutes and create a plan right now. From this book, identify the four primary marketing and promotion strategies you will employ over the next twelve months. Write it down *now*. There is tremendous power and clarity from physically writing your plan and your goals.

Here is a simple form to help you. Photocopy this page after you have written your plan. Carry it with you at all times and review it daily. This simple write and review process will help you stay focused on your promotional strategies.

Today's date:_____ This date next year_____

To be the Contractor of Choice I will promote myself with the following four Power Strategies:

Strategy #1 :_____from page #_____

My Plan:_____

Strategy #2:_____from page #_____

My Plan:_____

Strategy #3:_____from page #_____

My Plan:_____

Strategy #4:_____from page #_____

My Plan:_____

Strategy # 99

Make Your Work Your Passion.

Or better stated...make your passion your work. There is no substitute for living and working with excitement and passion. Passion is contagious and authentic. Passion is attractive. Customers will run to your door to be served by someone sincere and passionate about their work. The word will spread like wildfire that you are a person who is passionate about their business. Think about it. Who would you like to have working on your project? Someone who is careless and apathetic or a contractor who is jazzed by what they do? The most successful entrepreneurs in our society are those who look for opportunities to create new products and make existing products and services better. Make your work your passion.

Strategy #100

Become a "Walking Brochure."

Know *exactly* what service or product you provide. Be able to express the essence of what you offer in just a few strategically spoken words. Feel incredibly proud of what you do and what you offer. When people are attracted enough to come near you, make sure it's easy for them to say "Yes" to something you feel good about providing to them. Become a model for what you are selling. Customize what you are selling so that it fits you perfectly and it is a complete expression of your talents. Know what you want people to do, tell them to do it, and show them how to buy from you. People need direction. As a "walking brochure," all the information you need to promote yourself is in your brain. Be ready to use it and speak it at any moment.

Strategy #101

Just do it.

Nike made it famous. "Just do it." My father has said on many occasions, "There are two things in life, the 'Es' and the 'Rs,' Excuses and Results. Don't make excuses. Create results." There is no substitute for hard work and persistence. Learn and adjust along the way. The more you do it, the more you will want to do it right. I received this poem from my insurance agent.

You stick to the task until it sticks to you.
Beginners are many but Enders are few,
Honor, power, place, and praise,
Will come in time to the one who stays.
You stick to the task until it sticks to you,
You bend at it, you sweat at it, and you smile at it too,
And out of the bending, sweating, and smiling
Will come life's victory after a while.

Power Tip

Excellence is not a "sometime" event. Excellence is an every day thing. Your level of success is in direct proportion to your dedication to excellence.

— Paul Montelongo

In Conclusion
Ask, Ask, Ask, and Ask Again

As the author of a book on marketing and promotion, I would be remiss if I did not take my own advice. So, in an attempt to lead by example, I am going to ask, ask, ask, and ask again (see Strategy #3). I hope that you have enjoyed this book and more importantly, I hope that you will use this book. I know that if you employ just one strategy in this book fully, it will make a measurable improvement in the profitability of your business. So, what am I going to ask of you? There is power in the number three. I will ask three things of you now.

• **First**, send me the marketing and promotion strategies that have worked for you. Write me a letter, send me a fax or an e-mail with your creative tips and the experiences you have had with them. They can be strategies from this book or some of your own that are not included in this book. I am looking for more stories and examples to include in future books. I promise I will personally read each one that is sent. For your effort, I will send a copy of this book to a friend, associate, or colleague, free of charge and courtesy of you.

• **Second**, register on-line for my free electronic newsletter (see Strategy #48). Log on to www.ContractorOfChoice.com and sign up for the E-zine. Each month, you will receive strategies, tips, and coaching to promote yourself as the *Contractor of Choice*. The E-zine is free of charge and you may opt-in or opt-out at any time. Tell your friends about this too.

• **Third**, do something worthwhile for your community (see Strategy #64). There is no greater gift than to give of one's self. I would imagine that there are thousands of years of experience in the construction industry reading this book. If each one of us donates just a few hours a month to a worthy cause, collectively we can make a difference in our society (see Strategy #97). I would like you to seriously consider getting involved in Habitat for Humanity. This organization is perhaps the largest homebuilder in America and volunteers sponsor most of its work. There are those in our society less fortunate than us and we should do something to support them.

About the Author...
(Shameless Promotion Time
—See Strategy #12)

Nationally recognized speaker, author, and consultant to the construction industry, Paul Montelongo speaks at conventions and for corporations on how to become the *Contractor of Choice*. Paul is also a syndicated columnist. His articles are read by nearly a million people every month. Paul has built two multi-million dollar construction companies over the last 23 years. His companies have contracted with literally thousands of clients, from Fortune 100 companies to the private investor. He has employed hundreds of trade contractors and employees through the years.

Paul works with entrepreneurs in the construction industry to grow their business and increase their profits. He also works with related industries (banking, real estate, material distributors, etc.). If you would like more information about speaking, training, or consultation resources, contact Paul toll free at 1-866-494-1911 or send an email to paulspkr@swbell.net. Visit Paul on the web at www.PaulMontelongo.com. or www.ContractorOfChoice.com.

A final thought...

Marketing and promotion is the lifeblood of your business. As in any worthwhile endeavor, becoming the *Contractor of Choice* takes dedication and determination. The privilege that each of us has is to *make the choice* of taking our business to whatever level we desire.

The strategies presented in this book are by no means the last word in marketing and promotion ideas. Though these strategies have worked for me and thousands of other entrepreneurs, the extent to which you can invent more strategies is limited only by your imagination.

I welcome any ideas and strategies you use that may not be in this book. Also, if you would like coaching on how to implement any strategy in this book, feel free to contact me. Until we have the privilege of meeting in person, remember…"Success is *your* choice. Choose well."

Paul Montelongo

Suggested Reading

Beckwith, Harry. *Selling The Invisible*. Warner Books, New York, New York, 1997.

Blanchard, Ken and Johnson, Spencer. *The One Minute Manager*. Berkley Books, New York, New York, 1987.

Canfield, Jack and Hansen, Mark Victor. *The Aladdin Factor*. Berkley Books, New York, New York, 1995.

Carnegie, Dale. *How to Win Friends and Influence People*. Pocket Books, 1981.

Hill, Napoleon. *Think and Grow Rich*. Ballantine Books, New York, New York, 1937.

Leonard, Thomas J. *The Portable Coach*. Scribner Books, New York, New York, 1998.

Levinson, Jay Conrad. *Guerrilla Marketing: Secrets for Making Big Profits From Your Small Business*. Houghton Mifflin, Boston, Massachusetts, 1998.

Levinson, Jay Conrad. *Guerrilla Advertising: Cost-Effective Tactics for Small-Business Success*. Houghton Mifflin, Boston, Massachusetts, 1994.

Mackay, Harvey. *Swim With The Sharks Without Being Eaten Alive*. Ballantine Books, New York, New York, 1988.

Mackay, Harvey. *Dig Your Well Before You're Thirsty. The Only Networking Book You'll Ever Need*. Doubleday, New York, New York, 1997.

Pitino, Rick. *Success is a Choice. Ten Steps to Overachieve in Business and Life*. Broadway Books, New York, New York, 1997.

Ries, Al and Trout, Jack. *The 22 Immutable Laws of Marketing. Violate Them at Your Own Risk!* Harper Collins Publishers, New York, New York, 1993.

Robinette, Scott and Brand, Claire, and Lenz, Vicki. *Emotion Marketing. The Hallmark Way of Winning Customers For Life*. McGraw-Hill, New York, New York, 2001.

Order Form

Yes, I want more copies of this fantastic book to give to my friends, colleagues, employees, trade contractors, banker, accountant, and anyone else I may think of.

101 Power Strategies:
Tools to Promote Yourself as The Contractor of Choice

___copies @ $17.00 =_____ + S&H = $_____
Note: S&H = $3.50 per 1-5 books; for larger orders, call toll-free 1-866-494-1911.

Make Check Payable to Paul Montelongo Enterprises, Inc.

❏ Check here if you wish to receive information about workshops, consulting, or keynote presentations by Paul Montelongo for your business or professional association.

❏ Check here if you wish to receive Paul's **free** email newsletter. Receive tips, strategies, and coaching to promote yourself as the *Contractor of Choice*. Your email address is:

_____

❏ Mail, fax, or email to:
Paul Montelongo Enterprises, Inc.
1141 N. Loop 1604 E, Ste 105
PMB 407
San Antonio, Texas 78232
Fax: 210.494.3882 • email:paulspkr@swbell.net
Name:_____
Company:_____
Position:_____
City: _____State:_____ Zip:_____
E-mail: _____
Master Card / Visa #: _____
Expiration Date: _____
Signature:_____

Visit www.PaulMontelongo.com
or www.ContractorOfChoice.com
or call toll free 1.866.494.1911